Activity Book

Gillian Wolfe

Bellew Publishing London

First published in Great Britain in 1997
by Bellew Publishing Company Limited

Bellew Publishing Company Limited
8 Balham Hill, London SW12 9EA

Copyright © Dulwich Picture Gallery

Designed by Ray Carpenter
Illustrated by Linda Birch
Photography by Len Cross and Phil Polglaze
Muller Research Assistant Esmé Ward

Origination and Printing by
Supreme Publishing Services
Printed in Italy by Vallardi
Typesetting: Banbury Pre-Press

ISBN 1 85725 112 1

Contents

Foreword

Dulwich Picture Gallery and the Education Programme

Dulwich Picture Gallery is the oldest public art gallery in Britain, established in 1811. It houses a major collection of Old Master paintings including work by Rembrandt, Poussin, Rubens, Gainsborough and Canaletto which were originally bought for the King of Poland in 1790. The building, designed by the Regency architect Sir John Soane, is still regarded as one of the most successful examples of gallery design in Europe and has been frequently imitated in the design of new museums.

The Education Programme was started in 1984 by Gillian Wolfe. Her aim is to reach out to people with diverse cultural backgrounds and different levels of educational experience. She deliberately targeted youth and created a modern, innovative Education Programme which entices, entertains and educates.

The Education Department has won eight major awards for excellence in gallery education since 1987.

Introduction

To Children

Most children enjoy drawing.

The Magic Key to becoming a good artist is to:

DRAW   DRAW   DRAW

You <u>don't</u> need lots of flashy art materials to be good at art -

You just need to use your eyes - 👀 Children are often rather better than adults at noticing things.

Make a <u>habit</u> of carrying a sketch pad and pencil wherever you go - to jot down what you notice.

A tiny sketch pad will do,
many artists fill *hundreds*
of pocket sketch pads with their ideas.

Actual size of pad used by the famous artist
John Constable.

115 mm

83 mm

Look for this sign

your turn ✏️

It shows where to look for ideas
for *you* to try at home after
having looked at the paintings

The artwork examples in this book were made by primary school children between 7 and 11 years of age.

All the children's artwork made use of everyday materials readily available in the classroom and at home.

New Artwork from Old Masters

Looking at paintings carefully is an EXCELLENT way of getting ideas for your own artwork.

The KEY to using an artist's ideas for yourself is to LOOK LOOK and LOOK really hard! Then use what you see in a new way in your own art.

Try these NEW DESIGN ideas based on paintings:

IDEA 1 Enlarging a Detail

- Choose which small section or detail within a painting looks interesting to you.

- Use this as your starting point.

- ENLARGE this detail so that it fills up all your paper.

- This detail is now the whole of your new design.

- Colour it, perhaps add texture with pastel crayons, paint or collage and see how fresh and new your design looks.

Tiepolo *Fortitude and Wisdom*
or *Wisdom putting Ignorance to Flight*

Lely *Young Man as a Shepherd*

Rubens *St Barbara fleeing from her Father*

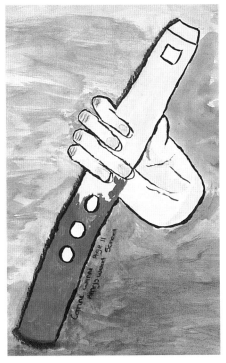

New Artwork from Old Masters

IDEA 2
A Detail as Starting Point

Choose a tiny portion of a
painting which interests you;
it could be a face, the door of a
house, an animal, a castle tower -
anything that takes your fancy.
(If you have a reproduction of
a painting, like a poster or
postcard, you could even cut out
this portion).

Copy just this small portion onto
your paper (or stick it down if
you have cut it out).

Carry on with your own design
added on around this original
detail, it can be as complicated or
simple as you like.

Now expand the drawing
to create whatever new picture
you like.

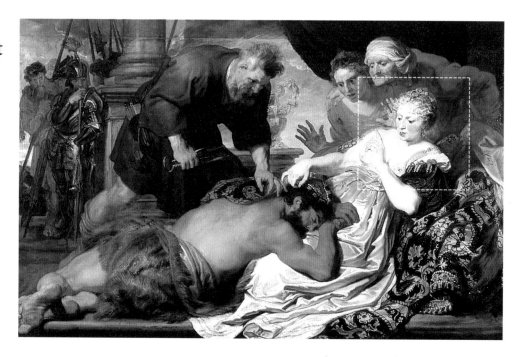

Anthony van Dyck *Samson and Delilah*

Murillo *Two Peasant Boys and a Negro Boy*

New Artwork from Old Masters

IDEA 3 Simplifying

You may find a picture that you like very much but you do not know how to begin making a drawing from it.

One way to find a starting point is to SIMPLIFY what you see.

Look at your picture and decide what you want to draw.

Then concentrate on drawing only the most important shapes - but keep them QUITE SIMPLE.

Leave out all the details - you can add these later if you want them.

Add colour, texture or background to your simplified shapes and you will have created a new piece of artwork that is all your own but based on another artist's idea.

Rubens *The Three Graces*

These simplified designs all capture a feeling of 'movement'.

your turn

In your sketchbook 'simplify' another artist's idea to make it your own.

Drawing Faces
Preparing for Portraits

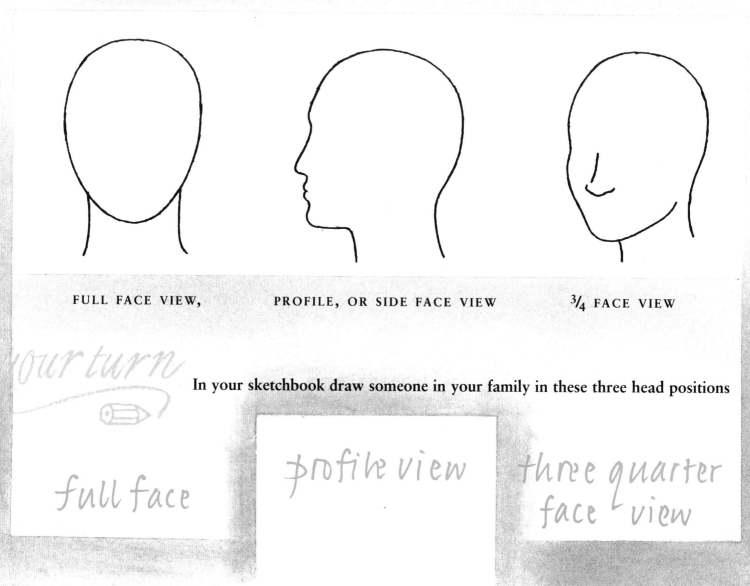

FULL FACE VIEW,   PROFILE, OR SIDE FACE VIEW   3/4 FACE VIEW

your turn

In your sketchbook draw someone in your family in these three head positions

full face   profile view   three quarter face view

Look at faces in photographs or illustrations in newspapers and books and copy them.

You can draw outlines over newspaper photos to get the feel of making face shapes.

which View?

Rembrandt *Girl at a Window (detail)*

Poussin *Rinaldo and Armida (detail)*

Piero di Cosimo *A Young Man (detail)*

Face Facts

Tips to give you a *head start* in drawing faces

Face Shape

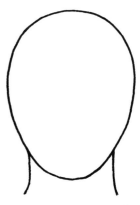

Faces are never really ROUND like a football!

Most faces are approximately egg-shaped.

Face Map

Use GUIDELINES to help you draw in the eyes and eyebrows, nose, mouth and ears. These will help you to draw them in the right place.

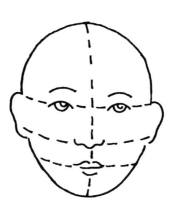

Face Space

Remember that foreheads are usually quite tall so don't start by putting the eyes right at the top of your oval - or you will be left with a lot of face space to fill and it will look all wrong!

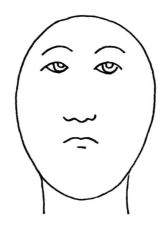

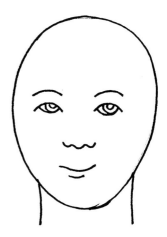

Eyes Right

Draw the eyes one half of
the way down your oval; this
guideline will help you fit
everything in and the face
will look in PROPORTION.

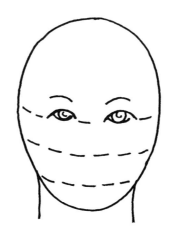
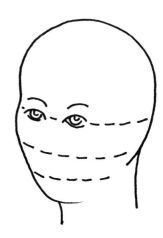

Hairy Topping

Remember that hair will usually
cover some of the top of the
forehead.

Draw these faces in your sketchbook then add guidelines in pencil to help you plan the face -
you can rub the guidelines out afterwards.

Drawing Faces Essential Extras

Ears

<u>Remember</u> - not to leave out ears - heads look odd without them!

<u>Remember</u> - not to draw the ears too small.

Look at people's ears (well, perhaps don't stare too hard!) - you will be surprised at how large they actually are. As a rough guide the top of the ear is level with the eyebrow and the bottom is level with the nose.

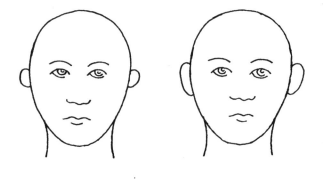

Necks

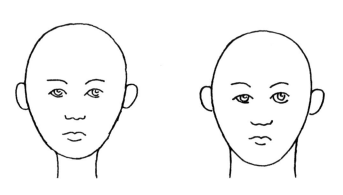

<u>Remember</u> a neck has to support a very heavy head, so it can't be weak and thin looking. Make your neck fairly sturdy and it will look right (in proportion) to the head.

Shoulders

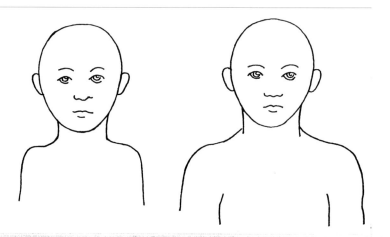

<u>Remember</u>, if you want to draw shoulders, then these are <u>much</u> wider than the head. Look at people and notice their shoulder width.

Supporting Cast Ears, Necks and Shoulders

1. Gainsborough *Mrs Moody and Two of her Children* (detail)

2. Knapton *Lucy Ebberton* (detail)

3. Netherlandish mid 1500s *The Fall of Man* (detail)

1

2

3

In your sketchbook, begin by drawing the head shape. Add good sized ears, a strong neck and sturdy shoulders. In time you will become skilled at drawing the head in PROPORTION.

Then you can add all the interesting ODD SHAPES and INDIVIDUAL EXPRESSIONS that will make your face come alive and begin to look like a real person.

3D Faces

Pancakes?

Heads and faces are not flat like pancakes. They are made up of interesting shapes - bumps, hollows and angles.

Shading

Artists make faces look '3 dimensional' by using SHADING.

The complicated name for this is the Italian word CHIAROSCURO, meaning 'light-dark'.

The simple name is MODELLING - not modelling with clay but with shading.

The GREAT MASTER of MODELLING with paint was the artist **Rembrandt**. This portrait by Rembrandt of his son Titus seems to loom out of the canvas, almost as if he were real.

This picture of an Unknown Man by Piero di Cosimo was once thought to be by Leonardo da Vinci, who is said to have invented the technique of MODELLING the face with light and shade.

Dolci *St Catherine of Siena*

Torn paper collage is a good way of showing the light and dark areas of the face.

Choose one of the paintings shown on this page.

Draw it and use pencil shading to show the shadows.

Getting the right balance of light and shade is a test of the artist's skill.

18

Rembrandt *A Young Man, perhaps the Artist's Son, Titus*   Piero di Cosimo *A Young Man*

Backgrounds

So, you have drawn and painted your portrait. NOW you need to decide what goes BEHIND it.

You COULD:

- Paint all one colour behind it;

- Let your brushstrokes show up in your background paint to add TEXTURE and interest;

- Add a HORIZON LINE and make it two colours behind;

- DESIGN your background so that it is an important part of the picture.

You can do this easily by adding some pattern or texture, as in these examples.

This rich and bold background design goes well with the flamboyant pose in the portrait.

Anthony van Dyck *George, Lord Digby, later 2nd Earl of Bristol*

What goes Behind

Reynolds *Mrs Siddons as the Tragic Muse*

A dotty background using light reflecting gold paint on black paper adds almost a starry night sky atmosphere.

Rembrandt *Jacob III de Gheyn*

No mistaking the artist here!
Try using letters or words in the background.

Tackling Texture

Use your PENCIL to make varied and interesting marks to create a feeling of different textures.

Your PENCIL can make lines, dots, smudges, squiggles, stabs, dashes and can do it thickly-thinly-smoothly-roughly.

Try this with different pencil types - notice the difference when you use an HB, 2B or 6B pencil.

In your sketchbook:

1) Use your pencil to try to recreate the texture featured in these details from paintings.

2) Make a collection of rubbings of different surfaces - how many can you find?

3) With colour, try sponging, stencilling and printing for interesting textures.

JABS

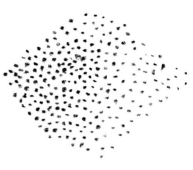

DOTS

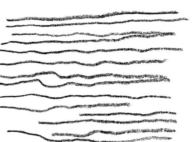

LINES

SQUIGGLES

SMUDGES

SHADING

HATCHING

DOUBLE HATCHING

Peeling tree bark

Pynacker *Landscape with Sportsmen and Game (detail)*

Glossy fur

Anthony van Dyck *Samson and Delilah (detail)*

Fluffy clouds

Att. to Cuyp *Cattle near the Maas, with Dordrecht in the distance (detail)*

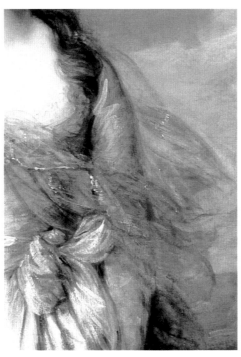

Choppy waves

Bakhuizen *Boats in a Storm (detail)*

Floating

Gainsborough *Mrs Moody and two of her Children (detail)*

Spiky twigs

Jan van Huysum *Flowers in a Vase (detail)*

Patterns hidden in Paintings

Patterns are to be seen all around you, you just need to get used to looking for them. Look at the way chairs, or cups or dishes are stacked, look at your pencils and pens or at bookshelves and you will see ready made pattern ideas, like these - from outside and inside Dulwich Picture Gallery.

British School *Joan Alleyn*

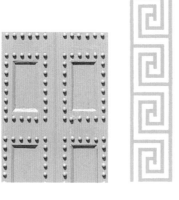

Paintings are also full of pattern. Notice pattern ideas when going round an art gallery.

In your sketchbook, use patterns from these paintings to make your own designs. Add colour to work up your idea into something quite new but <u>based</u> on a painting.

Neeffs I *Interior of a Gothic Church*

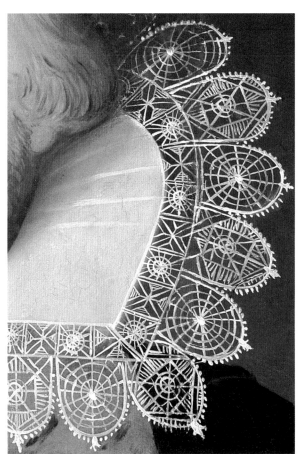

British School
'Old Mr Cartwright'

Canaletto *Old Walton Bridge over the Thames*

Near and Far

The Challenge

You want to draw a scene where some things are very NEAR to you and others FAR AWAY from you.

So ...
... somehow, you have to show DISTANCE between near and far.

How can you do it?

... by using PERSPECTIVE to trick the eye!

Helpful Hints for coping with Perspective

- Make things near to you **large**.
- Make things far away from you **smaller**.

- Make things near to you **bold and clear**.
- Make things far away **less clear and blurry**.

- Draw things far away **higher** up on your paper.
- Draw things near to you **lower** down on your paper.

- Colour things near to you **brightly**
- Make things far away **pale** with more blue tones.

- Make things like <u>roads or rivers</u> vanish into your <u>horizon line.</u>

Poussin *A Roman Road*

26

Perspective

Poussin's picture *A Roman Road* is a good example of PERSPECTIVE.

Here the PERSPECTIVE is simplified.

You try a PERSPECTIVE sketch in your sketchbook. Include a road and make it 'vanish' in the distance on the horizon. Add 3 trees and 3 people, large at the front and small at the back, medium sized in between.

Trees

In most LANDSCAPE pictures, TREES are an important ingredient.

Yet TREES can be TRICKY to draw and paint, they very easily turn out to look like 'blobs' and not the beautiful shapes they really are.

With a little preparation of LOOKING and SKETCHING your TREES can be TREEmendous!

lollipop - blob - or tree?

Try these tried and tested tree trips

Tree Trunks

Few tree trunks are really dead straight columns, most have an interesting character and shape, like the one in this painting by Verboom.

Verboom *Landscape with a Church (detail)*

Tree Barks

Look at the MARKINGS, COLOUR and TEXTURE of the bark. Some barks peel to leave marvellous patterns on the trunk.

Pynacker *Landscape with Sportsmen and Game (detail)*

Tree Outlines

Often you can tell what sort of tree it is just by looking at the outline shape.

Tree Leaves

Look at how the leaves grow - are they single, in pairs or like fingers - 5 to a 'hand' on one stem?
Are they densely packed together, or feathery looking?

Pynacker *Landscape with Sportsmen and Game (detail)*

Netherlandish mid 1500s *The Fall of Man (detail)*

Verboom *Landscape with a Church (detail)*

Tree Ideas

Go on a Tree Walk and sketch tree SHAPES. Name the trees if you can.

Collect leaves in the park; dry and press them and use them in collage.

Lie on the grass under a tree and look up - leaves make wonderful patterns against the sky.

Make designs based on the texture and pattern of rubbings of tree bark or on the shape of sprays of leaves.

Draw the same tree in winter and summer.

Changing Seasons

Teniers II *Winter Scene with a Man Killing a Pig*

David Teniers painted this picture to represent the season of Winter. Sometimes artists painted a series of pictures of the four seasons.

You could do the same - or you can make your own Seasons Calendar to hang in your room. Move the arrow to whichever season it is. If you like, you can make a much larger circle and divide it into twelve, and do a design for each month of the year.

Your seasons calendar will look something like this with your own designs on it. Use thin card, or glue your paper calendar on to card, attach a thin string loop for hanging and a split-pin paper fastener to fix the arrow in the centre.

Calendar

your turn

Draw or trace this onto card to make your Seasons Calendar.

The Key to 3D

Making things look solid

A drawing is quite flat, it is simply lines and marks on paper.

One of the tricks of drawing is to make things look SOLID, because that makes them look real and more lifelike.

One way to trick the eye and make things look solid or 3 dimensional (3D) is to use shading.

This is an OUTLINE drawing.

Now that shading has been added, which of these two bowls looks more solid and real?

Netherlandish mid 1500s
The Fall of Man (detail)

The solid Illusion

These apples and grapes look round and solid, not flat.

Michiel van Huysum
A Delft Bowl with Fruit (detail)

First, decide which side the LIGHT is coming from

Where will the LIGHT hit your drawing?

Wherever it is <u>not</u> light, draw in shadows.

At the very opposite side to where the light comes from, make the shadows darkest.

You should have a very LIGHT side and one that is very DARK, with gentle shading linking the two extremes.

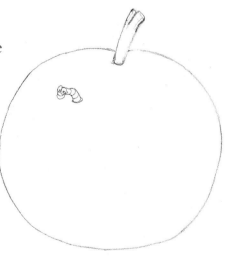

Try SHADING this outline drawing - copy it into your sketchbook and try to make it look THREE DIMENSIONAL and SOLID.

Draw a 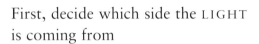 to show where the light is coming from.

Still Life

A STILL LIFE means a picture of things which do not move.

At first it meant mainly flower or fruit pictures, like this one by Michiel Van Huysum.

But now it can mean a group of any objects you choose.

Michiel van Huysum
A Delft Bowl with Fruit

Try grouping things like this for your own Still Life picture

your turn

Groups of all the same kinds of objects, such as model cars, teddybears or hats.

Objects which have SOMETHING TO DO WITH EACH OTHER in one arrangement e.g. all kitchen china or a few favourite toys, or garden tools, or delicious looking food.

▸

Things which all have SHINY SURFACES - the shine and reflections will make a really interesting drawing challenge.

Things with UNUSUAL TEXTURES such as straw, fur, lace, leaves - this will help improve your skill at making a flat surface come alive!

SPIKY, HARD THINGS which make good angles and sharp shapes e.g. thorny branches, tools, spiky shells.

ROUNDED FAT SHAPES that need a lot of shading to make them look 3 dimensional - such as grapes, apples, conkers and balls.

REMEMBER to put in a HORIZON line so that your ▸ STILL LIFE is not floating in space!

Do you <u>collect</u> anything?
If you do, put a group of your <u>collected</u> things together to make a 'still life' and draw them.

Serpents and Snakes

Netherlandish mid 1500s *The Fall of Man*

Choose one detail from a painting and use it in lots of different ways.

For example - **Take a Snake**

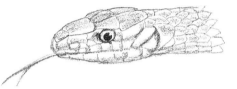

1. Enlarge one small part, in this case the head and make a new picture with it.

2. Make a curving swirly pattern made up of serpent shapes.

3. Make an interesting pattern or texture of snake scales.

4. Use shading to make it look 3D, slithery and real.

5. Add arms, legs, claws, wings, fire - turn it into a dragon!

Snake Mobile

Choose stiff-ish paper.

Draw a large circle on it.

At the centre point draw a snake's head.

Draw a spiral from the head to the edge of the circle.

Cut out the circle, colour or add patterns to both sides or foil scales to make it glisten.

Cut along the spiral lines.

Attach thread to head and hang up.

6. Make a 'snake' card bookmark.

7. Make a serpent mobile.

8. Draw a large decorated letter 'S' in a snake shape.

Creative Collage

Collage

from the French word 'coller'-
it means TO STICK TOGETHER.

Collage pictures are made by
glueing paper, cloth, feathers,
seeds, string, or anything you
like on to your background to
make a design.

Collage makes very exciting
artwork because -

- you can put odd materials
  together in a way never
  thought of before.

- you can create new textures.

- Using a painting for your idea,
  make your own collage.

- Your finished work may not
  look at all like your starting
  point but that doesn't matter -
  it will have become a new
  artwork of your own design.

Denning *Queen Victoria, aged Four*

Paper covered with writing, maths, scribbles and doodles has been usefully recycled here.

Jacob van Ruisdael *Landscape with Windmills near Haarlem*

Anthony van Dyck *Venetia Stanley, Lady Digby, on her Death-bed*

Tissue paper lightly sprayed with paint makes an interesting texture.

Collage Creations

Creased white paper handkerchiefs glued in between children's collage figures give a wintry snow and sky effect, to these collages based on Teniers *Winter Scene*.

Murillo *The Flower Girl*

Torn sugar paper mosaic forms the background, the hair is crumpled thin tissue strips and the flowers were sprayed and removed to leave an outline.

Make your own collage based on paintings.

Teniers II *Winter Scene with a Man Killing a Pig*

Colour Families

Look carefully at the colours in Old Master paintings - what do you notice about them?

The colours may look rather quiet to you because you are used to the bright ready - made paint colours available today.

When Old Master pictures were painted, artists had fewer colours available and these had to be made by hand by a studio apprentice.

Try some **Clever Colour Mixing** to see how many shades of one colour you can make. A picture painted in one **Colour Family** can look very attractive and subtle.

In this picture of *The Triumph of David* by Poussin, the colours are particularly clear and beautiful.

Children each chose one colourful character in the picture. They experimented with colour - mixing techniques to create designs based on Poussin's colour.

They made simple patterns by loosely drawing swirls and loops across the paper.

Each shape has been filled in with a different shade of the basic colour.

Hundreds of shades can be made by 'lightening' or 'darkening' or adding touches of any other colour to the first colour.

your turn

Try to make a 'COLOUR FAMILY' painting - (Change your water often so that colours do not become 'muddy').

Poussin *The Triumph of David*

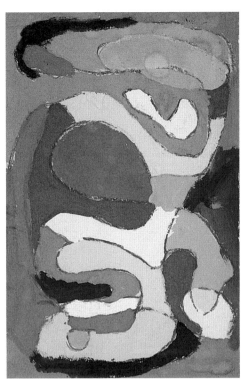
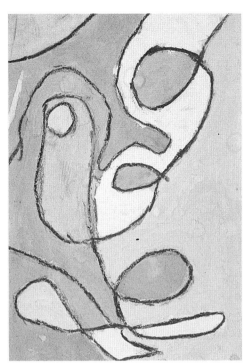

Pet Portraits

Perhaps you own a pet?
Perhaps you live near farm animals?
Perhaps you just like animals?

The Perfect Model

Animals make perfect models for budding artists because they are often in a resting position for long periods - long enough for you to take your time sketching them.

Even active animals must sleep sometimes, so seize your chance and reach for pencil and paper.

- Look carefully at an animal and try to capture some of the special sorts of MOVEMENTS it makes.

- Capture the particular SHAPE it takes when asleep.

- Practice drawing the TEXTURE of its fur, skin or feathers.

- Try to capture a particular expression or angle of the head.

Teniers II *The Chaff-cutter*

In your sketchbook, draw one of these

1) Portrait of my pet
   or
2) Landscape with farm animals
   or
3) (try this for a real challenge!)
   Animals in awkward positions

4) Look for animals in paintings and copy the way they have been drawn.

DAVID HARRIS

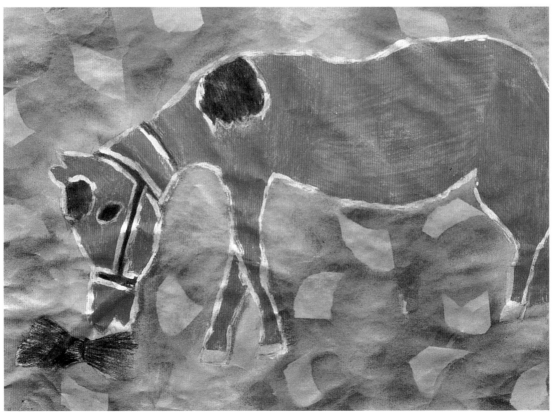

Self Portraits

Artists often paint their own self portrait.

RUBENS painted himself looking very grand in his finest nobleman's clothes - some artists are content to show themselves in work clothes.

REMBRANDT - one of the most famous artists of all, painted himself at least sixty times. In the days long before photographs, his self portraits were a record of his life, showing himself looking young and carefree, then middle-aged and wise and later old and ill.

In this self-portrait the young artist GREENHILL points to a drawing of himself. 300 years ago it was described as - 'greenhills pictur....dun by himselfe' showing how spelling and writing changes over time.

This self portrait by REYNOLDS is one of many that he painted to give away as presents to friends.

Greenhill *Self-portrait*

Try a self portrait - prop up a mirror and sketch yourself. Why not draw one for a present to someone in your family.

Reynolds *Self-portrait*

Children's Self Portraits

The Leopold Muller Estate

Leopold Muller was born in 1902 on the Austro-Czech border and died in England in 1988. He came to England as a refugee just before the Second World War, but sadly his wife and two daughters were unable to follow him and became victims of the Nazi Holocaust. On his arrival in London he opened a modest restaurant in the Edgware Road, and from this small beginning became a leading hotelier and restaurateur, acquiring many well known establishments throughout the country. In 1960 he created the De Vere Hotel chain which subsequently became a public company. De Vere rapidly expanded under Mr Muller's guidance and became the owner of, among others, the Grand Hotel's in Brighton and Eastbourne, the internationally renowned Mirabelle Restaurant in London and the Connaught Rooms.

Shortly before his death in June 1988, Mr Muller disposed of his business interests. Although he had acquired considerable wealth, he was a very private person who shunned publicity, preferring the quiet life and never allowing his photograph to be published. Having no surviving relatives, he bequeathed his estate to be applied for charitable purposes in England in appreciation of the refuge which had been given him by this country. It was his wish that the wealth that he had created should revert to his adopted country to do good for others.

The trustees of the Leopold Muller Estate have supported numerous charitable causes in this country with a total of more than 200 donations.

These have included projects devoted to the further education of young children and also in the assistance of museums and galleries associated with the National Heritage.

The trustees of the Leopold Muller Estate are delighted to support the new interpretation programme of the Education Department at Dulwich Picture Gallery.